Twenty One
Days of Praise

Published by Inner Peace Publishing

Cover Design by Tina Whitfield

©2013, Tina L. Whitfield

All scripture quoted is from the King James translation of the Holy Bible.

Library of Congress Cataloging-in-Publication Data has been applied for.

ISBN 978-0-692-47972-8

First Edition
First Printing
10 9 8 7 6 5 4 3 2 1

Inner Peace Publishing
P. O. Box 1231
Clayton, NC. 27528

Published and printed in the United States of America

i

Twenty One
Days of Praise

Dr. Tina L. Whitfield

~Table of Contents~

INTRODUCTION~1

PRAISE DAY ONE
~Praising Past Your Intellect~ 6

PRAISE DAY TWO
~Surrender~ 11

PRAISE DAY THREE
~Saturate~ 16

PRAISE DAY FOUR
~Bless His Name~ 21

PRAISE DAY FIVE
~Trust In Me With All Your Heart~ 27

PRAISE DAY SIX
~Praising Offense Away~ 34

PRAISE DAY SEVEN
~ Heart to Heart~ 40

PRAISE DAY EIGHT
~ The Refreshing Spirit of God~ 45

PRAISE DAY NINE
~ Renewed~ 50

PRAISE DAY TEN
~ Strength~ 56

PRAISE DAY ELEVEN
~ Forgive~ 61

PRAISE DAY TWELVE
~ Satisfied Praise~ 67

PRAISE DAY THIRTEEN
~ Praise for a Children~ 72

PRAISE DAY FOURTEEN
~Dance Praise~ 78

PRAISE DAY FIFTEEN
~God Has Birth A Blessing Inside Of You~ 83

PRAISE DAY SIXTEEN
~ Frustrated Purpose~ 88

PRAISE DAY SEVENTEEN
~Praising Through Fear~ 92

PRAISE DAY EIGHTEEN
~ Walk With God~ 97

PRAISE DAY NINETEEN
~Weeping~ 103

PRAISE DAY TWENTY
~ Hidden Treasures~ 108

PRAISE DAY TWENTY ONE
~ It's All About Him~ 113

~21 Days Of Praise~

Introduction

There are many believers who are walking around not exercising the gifts that God has given them. Praise is a gift that is underutilized in the body of Christ. Let everything that hath breath praise the Lord. Praise ye the Lord (Psalm 150:6 KJV). So if you are not praising God, you are missing a very important part of your Christian walk. You are missing the relationship that encourages your spirit and soul towards the Lord.

There are some who don't see the importance of praise. Your praise is so important that God inhabits your praise. *Psalm 22:3 KJV But thou art holy, O thou that inhabitest the praise of Israel.* This means that He holds the praise close to Him, He keeps it, and He releases your blessing upon you like showers of blessings. I am not saying that if you don't praise you will not be blessed.

However, why neglect such a wonderful piece of your salvation not praising. Israel, in the above scripture, represents the people who serve God. If you say that you love the Lord, praise God. Praise is important for many reasons. Your praise waters your soul as the rain waters the earth. We need the rain to water the earth to help the production of food, water, and the survival of our existence. Praise is a good indication to God that you believe and trust in Him.

How do you Praise? In the book of Hebrew, praise is depicted as the wringing of the hands, praise, shout, and giving thanks. Praise is an act that communicates that you are building and confirming your relationship with God. Positive reinforcement, encouragement, and accolades are all forms of praise. Praise should be a daily event, just as prayer. Praise is often neglected because it is not seen as important as prayer, faith, obedience, and trust among Christians.

Praise is associated with a popular cliché that praises go up and blessings come down. The time that you are waiting upon your blessing may be difficult when it appears that nothing is happening, and you feel that God has not heard your prayer and seen your faith. I heard a minster call this the "Mean-time." Some of us have been waiting so long that that you feel that the Lord has forgotten you. During the "mean-time," it is your time to praise God. Praise is the water that pushes your faith, prayer, and confessions into manifestation.

Praising during the meantime is proliferation that has to happen even when you are at a give up point. You have to stir up the spirit realm to let God know that you mean business. God moves when you move. There are those who are waiting on God, and God is waiting on you. Know that when you move and stir up the spiritual realm that your adversary is coming to attack you to get you off course. You have to put on the whole armor of God and stand and know that the word of God is your shield.

You have to make an informed decision to take God at his word and stand on it. If you are still praying to God, asking Him the same question, you are not walking in faith. He heard you the first time. *Isaiah 59:1 Behold, the Lord's hand has not shortened that he cannot save; neither his ear heavy that it cannot hear.* When we praise it brings us closer to God and God closer to us.

Think of this for a moment. When we see our love ones, associates, or even a stranger doing something good or outstanding, it is normal to give them a compliment or an encouraging word. If we see someone cry, or if they are discouraged about an issue, we tend to point out all of their wonderful qualities that they should be proud of.

Praise is the same thing, except, we are praising our Lord for all the wonderful things that He has done, and is doing in our lives. This morning when you woke up, was there any doubt in your mind that you would not see the sun? People often take for granted that each day is a gift. Everyday is a reason just to stand in the presence of God and be grateful for the air in your body. I can't say it enough. Praise the Lord just because you woke up.

When children cry, adults run to see what has happened. God sees us as children, his children, when we praise Him, He comes. Can you imagine how He must feel, when his name is being called, and when He arrives you are just giving Him thanks? You are becoming closer to God when you praise. You are dwelling with the Lord. He sees you, and He appreciates you. He is all knowing and all loving. How great is our Lord? What a mighty and awesome God we serve. He is magnificent in all things. Your praise ushers in the presence of the Lord.

Will you trust God for the next 21 days to see a change in your praise and love for the Lord? Settle this in your mind that you will not give up. The next 21 days you will focus on an agape love journey with the Lord. Make a decision today that you will praise God regardless of any distractions that may occur to hinder you from praising God.

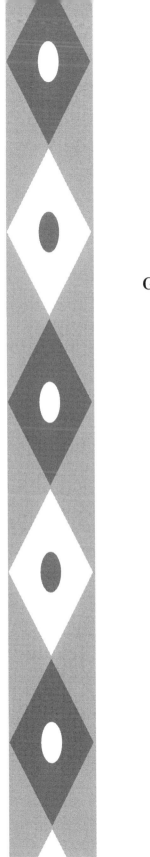

Give God The Praise

Praise Day One

~ Praising Past Your Intellect~

K nowledge is power depending on how that knowledge will benefit others or yourself. You need your intellect to take a test, get into a university or college, or to perform certain work related tasks. It has been instilled from the beginning of time that if you know more you will make more money. God wants you to get wisdom and understanding to prosper in life.

One beautiful Sunday afternoon, I was sitting on the porch with Pastor JeSonya Hargrove. We discussed the depth of intellect and how it may affect a productive praise life. When we evaluated the word intellect, we were astounded at the findings. Webster dictionary stated that intellect is the power of knowing as distinguished from the power to feel and to will: the capacity for knowledge.

The second definition stated, "the capacity for rational or intelligent thought especially when highly developed." Both of those definitions have depicted the need for knowledge. The question now becomes, am I able to use my same intellect to get in the presence of God? The answer is no; God is a spirit and to understand the spirit you must go beyond your mind set and believe in the spirit realm.

John 4:10 God is a spirit: and they that worship him must worship him in spirit and in truth. Praise is spiritual, and if you are unable to separate your intellect from your spirit, your connection will only be one of carnality and not of truth. God needs you to remove yourself and become a part of Him. It doesn't matter how intelligent you may be, how many degrees you have, or your title at work.

Your intellect can hinder your praise. If you don't lay your intellect to the side, when you are praising God, you may try to rationalize why you are praising a God that you cannot see. Reading his words daily will penetrate your heart and feed your spirit of whom God really is. Your mind is such a powerful instrument, and if you don't read God's word, you will come up with your own ideology of whom God is instead of God saying whom He is. There isn't any way to truly conceptualize who God is in your intellect. You have to allow God's wisdom to guide you with understanding who He is through his spoken word.

Spiritual intelligence allows you to perform in the spiritual realm. In *1 Samuel 17*, David was given instruction by God how to defeat the giant Goliath. In the natural, a rock and a sling is a toy to most kids. Most of us would have thought immediately that this little man was inviting death and missed God's instruction. David listened to God in his spirit and not with his intellect.

Don't allow your intellect to get in the way of God speaking to you. The word Intellect is broken into three sections (In-tel-lect.). The IN represents your inner thoughts and perceptions in intellect, TEL represents what you are saying to yourself, and the LECT represents the lecture you give in reference to whom God is from your perception. This is the carnal thinking of man. So don't let your In-Tel-Lect get in the way of your praise.

Today, your praise should be, God, for the next 21 days I decrease my intellect and allow you to take over and direct me in all my ways. Lord today is the beginning of revitalization in my thinking towards you. I'm not looking for a restoration, but a revitalization of who you are and what I need to do to please you. Today Lord, I lift my hands, eyes, and ears up to you.

I give you all of me without conditions Lord. Remove the layers that have kept me from hearing, seeing, and truly praising you. I want my relationship with you to be without condition. I want to come in the throne room naked (exposed spiritually) and with expectancy to just love you. My revitalization can only take place in front of you.

I am the clay that is set before you to mold at your will. I stand before you Lord hungry for your love and instruction. Today, your praise represents how you stand humble in front of God to let Him know you will not allow your intellect to dictate your praise today. You will not over think this process. Just allow the words of adulation for the Lord to flow freely from your lips. Don't over think this process.

Tell the Lord what He means to you. Mentally peel back the layers that have kept you from truly praising God. Put your degrees to the side, your mama's interpretation of who God is, your friends belief system that praise isn't necessary, and your daddy's thoughts that God isn't a right now God. Let your carnal thinking die and take your mind to a place of beauty and peace.

Talk to God as if you are talking to one of your best friends. Believe it or not He is the friend that will stand with you in any storm, fight your battles, and never leave you. He is the friend that asked, "How can I help you?" Praise His Holy name! Praise the God that laid down his life for you. Put your intellect to the side, raise your hands, fall to your knees, lift up your voice, open your ears, and let your heart rejoice. Enter into his presence. Tell God how important it is to you that He took the time to spend it with you.

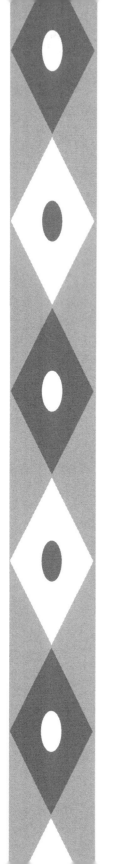

Think the way Jesus wants you
to Think.

Praise Day Two

~Surrender~

Today, picture yourself in front of the Lord kneeling down before Him. Be honest with the Lord, Tell Him your fears, likes, dislikes, desires, and if you are angry with Him. Surrendering yourself is giving God the very intimate part of your being. Your praise is the beginning of your journey of learning to trust God and build your most intimate relationship with Emmanuel.

Surrendering to the Lord is submitting yourself to God's authority. *Psalms 18:44 As soon as they hear of me they shall obey me: the strangers shall submit themselves unto me.* The Lord is saying that once your eyes are open to Him, you are able to hear His voice, and be obedient to His words. If this is your first time attempting to praise God, you may have some difficulty understanding how to praise Him.

Praise is as easy as opening up your mouth and saying, I love you, Lord. You may want to start off by just being honest with God, that you need help with praise. Make a list of things that you are grateful for having, the unpleasant moments, and things that you are completely over in your life. Once you see the list, you have written the reasons to praise God.

Yes, praise Him for not only the good, but those unpleasant moments in your life. Although, it may not have felt good, you made it through that moment. God deserves the praise in the midst of trouble and joy. Praising God is never contingent upon your feelings. Praise is your gift to God and it should never be taken advantage of.

If you take the time to think about it, His love, grace, and mercy aren't contingent upon you doing right all the time. He blesses you because you belong to Him. His love isn't fickle at all. Your love for Him should be unconditional as well. Your praise is informative to the Lord.

You are praising Him for the seen and the unseen blessings in your life. *Psalm 8:11; sing praises to the Lord, which dwelleth in Zion: declare among the people his doings.* Always walk with thanksgiving and know that the Lord is with you. Today, change your routine. Whatever it is that you like to do the most, don't do it, and replace that activity with praise.

For example, I love to talk on my phone. Instead of talking on the phone, I talk to the Lord during that time I am normally on the phone. God wants you to share with Him how you feel towards Him. Tell Him how wonderful He is, and thank Him for the great opportunities that you are expecting today. Walk in the authority of expectancy when you praise the Lord.

The Lord is so loving, kind, gentle and giving. Why not praise Him today with surrendering yourself to his will? *Psalm 9: 1-2 I will praise thee, O Lord, with my whole heart: I will shew forth all thy marvelous works. I will be glad and rejoice in thee: I will sing praise to thy names, O thou most High.* At this moment look up at the sky, regardless of what your circumstances are, throw your hands up to heaven, and speak with a confident, loud voice, exalting the Lord's wonderful works in your life. You speak in the authority that God has ordained you to walk in.

Example: Lord, I just want to thank you. I'm so glad that I was able to get in touch with you this morning. God I'm glad that you allowed me to see another beautiful day. Today, I wanted to tell you how much I love you and adore you. You are my beginning and end. You sent the birds to sing to me this morning. Lord, today I just wanted you to know that I am listening for a word from you. Lord you are the air that I breathe. I thank you for clearing the path on my way to work. You are a wonderful God. I woke up with a peace that passes all understanding.

The book of Psalms is a terrific place to start to learn how to praise God. The book of Psalms is your praise anthem for anyone who is having problems with finding something to praise about. The book of Psalms also instructs you on how to praise the Lord. Praise is surrendering your will unto the Lord and letting Him know that you will obey his will and not be led by your own will. God's will is first in your life.

You understand that God is your Emmanuel, Jehovah Jireh, and Jehovah Nissi. Praising God should never be optional. Giving your life to Jesus was the best decision you made. The next best decision is to praise God daily just because He forgave you of your sins, and not once will He remind you of what you did. What an awesome God we serve? Surrender to Him today, He is waiting.

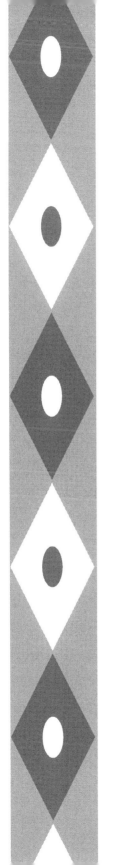

Walk in HIS will

Praise Day Three

~ Saturate~

S aturate yourself today in the word of God. Make your day about Him. Steal moments today to hear the word of God. Absorb yourself in his music, reading, and praise. Saturating yourself in the things of God, keep God on your mind. This allows your heart, mind, and soul to prosper!

3John 2, Beloved, I wish above all things that thou mayest prosper and be in health, even as thy soul prospereth. Prospereth means to succeed in reaching, in this scripture. God wants the believer to prosper in all your goals. You represent Him, and representing Him means that you are prosperous in all things.

Praise is so important, but it is often taken for granted by believers. Believers often neglect praise because they feel that prayer should be enough. If you believe this, you are not incorrect, but you are incomplete. Although, prayer is a form of communication with God, He wants you to pray daily. Prayer is a very different type of communication that people are petitioning God to intervene on their behalf or interceding for someone.

Praise communicates your love and adoration for God. Although, an effective prayer warrior always acknowledges God's gifts, before requesting God to heal, save, and perform miracles in your life. Praise allows you to appreciate the blessings that God has given you, by thanking Him. Praise summons God's attention and He adores your praise. Praise is another form of communication that allows God to know that you love Him, and you recognize how important God's presence is in your life. Taking time out to acknowledge Him in all your ways is significant to the Lord.

Think of a new born baby, and how that infant communicates through crying with his/her parent that something is wrong. Once the infant begins to cry, the parents immediately begin to console the child. The parent will pick up the crying child to comfort the child, or give the child a bottle, or sing to the child to attempt to discover what may be the problem with the child. When God's children cry out to God with praise, He turns to us with his absolute attention.

He is now listening to how you are loving Him. He takes your praise and captures it as a picture. Others will start to notice how good God is to you by the joy that you exude in your life. This is His gift returned unto you for your praise. When you take time to praise, you don't have time to complain.

God allows others to see the blessing in your life when you take the time to give Him the praise. Blessings are in many forms. People may see a peace in your life that hasn't always been there. You may start to experience a different outlook on how you perceive the world in which you live. People that use, to annoy you may become more tolerable, and the work place may become more enjoyable.

Show Him that you trust Him by indulging in the word. Meditate on the word. Engulf your life today with scriptures, songs, and praise. Take your lunch time and just thank Him for how terrific He is. You don't have to wait until Sunday when you have today. Remember, praise is a lifestyle, and today your life is a representation of whom you serve.

Give God your undivided attention. You play a vital role with your manifestation of God's gifts in your life. You have to sing with a loud voice of thanksgiving. Today, I challenge you to sing praises unto the Lord. *Psalm 96:1, O sing unto the lord a new song, sing unto the Lord, all the earth.* Allow a song to help you praise the Lord. Today, sing your favorite songs and dedicate the song to the Lord.

Today your only strategy is to love on the Lord. Find your voice and love on the Lord today. If you have asked God for

18

something and you are waiting for those things to manifest in the natural, don't give up, just praise Him in the meantime until you see what you have asked for. *Ezekiel 12:28, Therefore say unto them, Thus saith the Lord God; There shall non of my words be prolonged any more but the word which I have spoken shall be done, saith the lord God.* He said, "none of my words be prolonged". Believe that you will see the manifestation of what you have asked.

Praise brings peace in the midst of your waiting. During the time that you are waiting on the Lord, you should be busy doing the will of God. Work while you are waiting on Him. Don't let procrastination kill your dreams. God will add unto you what you need when you need it.

Absorb yourself in Him. When people talk to you, do they see God in you? Who is represented first when people meet you? Ask yourself is your light shining when you walk in the room? Often people think they are representing God, when only they are representing their own flesh. A bad attitude is not a representation of God.

Absorb yourself in Him to show others the right way to a loving and kind God. God is love, and, if you are not walking in that love, are you truly absorbing yourself in his word. It is difficult at times to walk in love when someone may be provoking you, but true love looks past it, and forgives. Absorb yourself in Him, so that the world does not absorb itself in you.

Read Daily

Praise Day Four

~ Bless His Name~

Blessing the name of the Lord edifies God. *Deuteronomy 5:10 And shewing mercy unto thousands of them that love me and keep my commandments.* Blessing the name of the Lord is loving Him and obeying his word. Today, you will position yourself to keep your mind on the Lord and bless his name. Keeping his commandments allows you to keep your mind on Him.

Blessing His name daily reminds you of whom He is to you. Blessing His name at all times keeps you in His will and not your will. If you bless the Lord how will you have time to work against His plan for your life? Let His words, which is the word of God, to continually come out of your mouth. God wants you to praise Him throughout the day with the word of God.

Your words shape your environment. If you begin to shape your environment with praise, you are shaping your relationship with the Lord. Blessing His name communicates to the Lord that you are committed to the relationship with Him. When you bless the Lord you adore Him, and in return He blesses those that bless His name. Psalm 103:1 *Bless the Lord, O my soul: and all that is within me, bless his holy name.*

Authentic praise towards the Lord is essential to forming a relationship with the Lord. The scripture says, *Psalm 103:1 Bless the Lord, O my soul, and all that is within me!* Authenticity is important to the Lord. Praising God from within and not pretending to praise Him, is essential not just for you, but for God. His grace and mercy abound in your life.

There is nothing that you can do to prevent His grace and mercy from abounding. Grace and mercy are gifts that you obtain when you gave your life to Jesus. When you continually praise Him you are forever increasing with hearing from the Lord. God said that He knew you before you were formed; you are transparent to Him. He knows when you are praising Him in truth and authenticity.

The book of Joshua depicts praise in such a wonderful and meaningful way. God instructed Joshua on how to take the city of Jerico. Joshua 6:3-5. In verse 5 God said, *And it shall come to pass, that when they make a long blast with the ram's horn, and when ye hear the sound of the trumpet, all the people shall shout with a great shout; and the wall of the city shall fall down flat, and the people shall ascend up every man straight before Him.* This is important, God didn't instruct Joshua to take a hammer and tear the walls down. The walls could only come down with a great shout. Ask yourself, "Who comes to a battle with a praise?" Christians should always approach everything with praise.

If the walls of Jerico fell with a shout or praise, what would happen if you praised God about your depression, lack, unforgiveness, your inability to move the glass ceilings in your life, sex sins, or anything that is keeping you from moving forward in life. All you have to do is praise God to begin the process to move from a stagnated state to a productive state. God's grace is his unmerited favor that is bestowed upon the believers.

Unmerited favor is more precious than anything that you can try to conceptualize in the human mind. Unmerited favor is never understood by the unbeliever, but the believer has the opportunity to tap into the grace of God with authentic praise. Praise represents your love for the Lord. Picture standing before the Lord each time you are awake. How would you bless his name?

You would start with simplicity. First start your authentic praise with thanksgiving. When entering into the presence of God, you always give thanks. Start today with, "Lord you are so wonderful, that you are giving me another opportunity to grace your presence. I Bless your Holy name. You are the Holy of Holiness. You are beautiful Lord and just. You are my beginning and my end. Today, I will bless your name! No one can love me the way that you do." Bow down before Him and give yourself totally to Him.

Blessing his name isn't difficult. Think about how you give others compliments on their clothing, job performance, grades in school, or any accolades that allow others to know that you appreciate them and you are proud of their accomplishments. Now you give God all the accolades for being God. You can find a reason to bless Him. You are able to read the print on this page, that is a reason right there to bless his Holy name.

Don't take for granted that blessing the Lord is not important. The opportunity to bless his name should be a joyous occasion. An occasion that should be looked upon with anticipation, and enthusiasm when entering into the presence of the Lord. Always, imagine yourself standing before Him when you are praising Him. Envision Him wrapping his loving arms around you, and whispering how much He loves you, when you stand before Him.

Remember, He sees your heart! He knows what you want before you speak it. For those of you who say, "Why do we have to say it when He knows it?" Words shape your environment.

What you speak shows up in your life when you speak. Stop speaking what you do not have, because He that dwells inside of you, is greater, wiser, richer, and will assist you with your desires.

He is greater than what you don't have. When you bless the Lord, you are speaking blessings in your Life. The devil hears you, and He knows if you praise the Lord, he cannot compete with the Lord's grace. He can't compete with the Lord. Your praise is a weapon in the spirit realm that shows up in your physical world. *Jeremiah 32:18 Thou shewest lovingkindness unto thousands, and recompensest the iniquity of the father into the bosom of their children after them: the Great, the Mighty God, the Lord of hosts, is his name.*

.

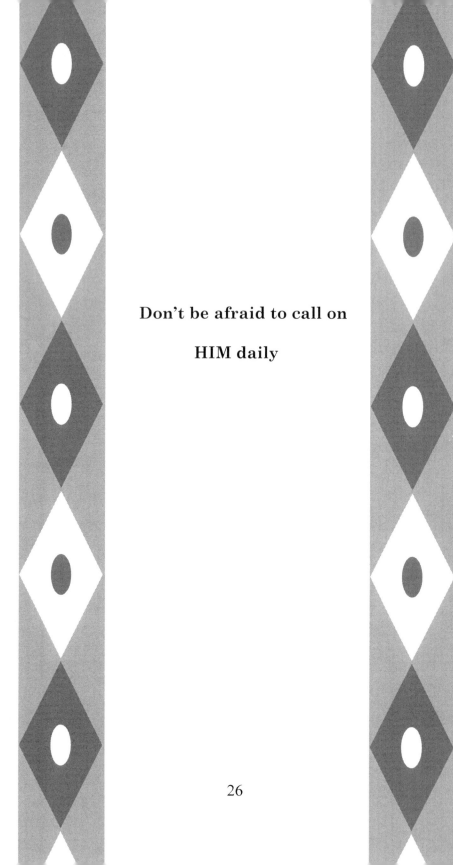

Don't be afraid to call on

HIM daily

Praise Day Five

~ Trust In Me With All Your Heart~

Trusting in people can be a challenge for the most perspicacious individual. Trust is normally earned if you perceive it carnally. Today, make a covenant with the Lord that you will trust Him regardless of what may happen in your life. This is not easy for those who believe you have to build trust. God is reliable, accountable, and trust worthy but when you have a problem trusting, you will not believe that you can trust Him.

2 Samuel 22:3 The God of my rock; in him will I trust: He is my shield, and the horn of my salvation, my high tower, and my refuge, my savior; thou savest me from violence. God is your strength and in Him you will obtain the will to completely rely on Him for all your needs. Today, your praise should be guided with entering his presence with the voice of thanksgiving. God is omnipotent in your life.

Once you surrender yourself to the Lord, trusting Him is an attribute that you have to build with the help of the Lord. Today, start your praise with, "God you are my truth, you have my heart, and in you I live, and in you I trust, and in you I abide hidden in your secret place. I'm surrounded by your love and kindness."

Trusting and relying on the Lord doesn't come as easy as some Christians will make you believe. There are many who say they love the Lord, but they do not trust in Him to change anything in their lives. If you take the initiative to praise the Lord today and every day, saying that you trust Him, you will begin to see a difference in your love walk with the Lord.

The death of Jesus is an exemplary example of trust among the disciples' reactions when they were informed that Jesus has risen from the grave. Jesus prepared the disciples for the coming of his death. He told them that He would rise after three days. Although they knew this, did they really trust what He said? When Jesus appeared the disciples believed only because they had seen Him.

This reaction is still prominent today in believer's lives. They only believe in what they see. People live in fear that God will not supply all of their needs. Believers are still trying to do everything in their own power instead of trusting God to take care of their issues. *1 Peter 5:7 Casting all your care upon him; for He careth for you.* Trust God enough to assist you out of your troubles. You have nothing to lose but everything to gain by trusting in Him.

Think about an adversity that you endured. Did you think that God placed that adversity in your life? If you answered, "Yes," you are mistaken. We do not go through adversity, because there is a lesson that you need to learn. *John 16:33 These things I have spoken unto you, that in me ye might have peace. In the world ye shall have tribulation: but be of good cheer; I have overcome the world. You have a real enemy and his name is Satan.*

Satan wants you to go through a tremendous amount of adversity. *2 Samuel 22:31 As for God, his way is perfect; the word of the Lord is tried: He is a buckler to all them that trust in him.* God is saying in that He is divine and although persecution comes, if you hold on to Him; his word will not fail you. He is the shield that will protect you from your enemy. The enemy wants you to give up on God! Trust that He is your shield in your life. He has you hidden in a secret place of protection.

When the believer doesn't trust the Lord, you are not obedient in your walk with God. *Job 36:11 If they obey and serve Him, they shall spend their days in prosperity, and their years in pleasures.* Start trusting God today. Let Him know that today is a new beginning in your life and you are committed to trusting in Him.

Today, think of something that you know you need assistance in, but in your own ability you know that you are powerless to get the task completed without the Lord. Below, I have given an example of how I had to trust the Lord for a supernatural outcome. I needed help, and only God could assist me.

One Christmas I was really struggling financially and I had just gotten a job three months earlier. I had a tremendous amount of expenditures from being unemployed. I had a hundred dollars to purchase all of my Christmas presents. This may not seem like a problem to most people, but I like to give and I know everyone Jesus is the reason for the season. I needed to stretch that money in a supernatural way. I lifted my eyes up to the Lord, and I began to praise the Lord for the $100 dollars. I praised God as if I had a thousand to spend. I got so excited about my $100 dollars, and I placed my trust in the Lord like never before. After, I praised God, I was then ready to shop. I had my list and as I walked in the store, I said, "Jesus, hold my hand and let's go shopping." I talked to God and I reminded Him how He turned two fishes into plenty in the Bible. I told the Lord how much I loved Him and how much I trust Him. I also reminded Him how He took care of me when I was unemployed. As the Lord and I walked into the store, I had a couple of glances because I was still talking to the Lord. I asked the Lord to work a special miracle today. I grabbed my cart and with a smile on my face I began the best shopping experience that I had ever experienced in my life. God worked wonders with my $100. I got the most amazing deal. Over 85% of my items I needed were on clearance. The largest item on the list was marked down to $40 dollars. I walked out of the store paying $97.00 with a cart full and $3 dollars to spare. Trust God, Trust God, with all of your heart. He is an on time God.

In the book of Joshua a harlot spoke to the two men who came to make a report to Joshua about the city of Jericho. She hid the men on the roof of her home. She said in Joshua 2:10. *For we have heard how the Lord dried up the water of the Red sea for you, when ye came out of Egypt: and what ye did unto the two kings of the Amorites, that were on the other side of Jordan, Si'horn and Og, whom ye utterly destroyed.* She told them that she knew that the Lord had given Jericho to them.

People will hear how God has delivered you out of adversity. Your life will speak volumes of how much you trust in God. A harlot woman trusted only by hearing of the goodness of the Lord. Once you start giving your praise report about how God has been so good to you, people will want the same God that you serve. You are the light in the world, so shine brightly in everything that you do.

Give God your praise today! Trust in Him to support you in all your endeavors and He is faithful in his word. Believe and trust in the Lord! Your trust will only increase in your praise and obedience to God! If you do nothing, please expect nothing to change in your life.

God will not Fail You

Praise Day Six

~ Praising Offence Away~

P raising God when you are offended is an enormous task when your heart is full of anger and bitterness. Clearing your heart and mind is essential during this time. You certainly do not want anything to hinder your praise time with the Lord. Remember that you are transparent and the Lord knows when you are truly spending time with Him or just passing time.

Hosea 5:15 I will go and return to my place till they acknowledge their offence, and seek my face: in their affliction they will seek me early. Never allow offence to hinder your praise. You can control your emotions; you have the ability to change your attitude. Making a slight attitude adjustment, affects your personality immediately. Forgiving those whom have offended you is courageous.

34

Examine Cain and Able's relationship with God. Able worshiped and praised God with his best harvest. God acknowledged Able's good works, and Cain became very offended with his brother instead of examining himself. Cain did not honor the Lord as his brother did with the best of his harvest. Cain was very angry, and killed his brother because he was offended that God said, "Able gave Him the best of his harvest."

If Cain had taken the time to make an attitude adjustment by critically weighing the consequences of his actions, he would have first acknowledged that he needed to blame himself for choosing not to praise God properly. Secondly, Cain should have repented to the Lord instead of hiding from Him when he killed his brother. He took the cowardly way out, and killed his brother because he perceived that his brother was the problem.

Make sure that your offence isn't something that you created, and you are displacing your negative emotions on another individual. Sometimes looking in the mirror is difficult when the person looking back looks identical to you. Grow up and stop pointing the finger at others. Judge yourself first.

Thirdly, don't ever think you can conceal yourself from God. God is omnipotent! Placing negative emotion aside and giving God his attention is a win/win for everyone but the enemy.

Positioning yourself to praise intimidates the enemy but gives God the exaltation that is due to Him. Thank God for the challenge. This demonstration of praise during your affliction speaks volumes about your character. Start your praise today with, "Heavenly Father, thank you for delivering me from the hands of my enemy. Thank you for assisting me with casting down imaginations that deviate from the word of God."

Thank you God, for loving me through the awkward moments in my life, although offense presented itself, I forgive the person, and I forgive myself for allowing someone else's behavior to dictate my emotions in Jesus name I pray, amen. God expects you to praise during your struggles and your successes. He knows that you view Him blameless in adversity, and in the midst of trouble, you have armored yourself from the crown of your head to the souls of your feet with the word of God.

Be confident in your praise to see the victory in your future. *John 16:1 These things have I spoken unto you, that ye should not be offended.* Offence hinders the growth of the believer towards the word of God. Some believers are challenged with repetitive problems that continue to influence how they react to certain incidents that keep you away from achieving Gods' best in your life.

If you continue to murmur and complain, you are not practicing the word of God. *Psalm 141:3 Set a watch, O Lord, before my mouth; keep the door of my lips.* Pursing ontological epistemic agility towards positive speaking will enhance your life. Be careful when speaking negative word in your environment, you do not want to hinder your praise with a negative attitude. Remember your words shape the life that you are living. Your words are powerful! This bears repeating, "you shape your environment with your words." Be careful with the words that you speak into the environment.

Don't say, "I am dying to see you!" Change it to, "I'm excited to see you." Simple and small changes in your speech change your view of your world. Negative speech brings negative things into your life. Speak life and watch great and wonderful things happen in your life. Removing negative speech promotes positive praise, which aligns the believer with the abounding grace to continue to praise the Lord in truth.

Understand that praising God will assist you with maturing in your love walk with others, even when they offend you. You will see that you are able to forgive faster when you continue to stay in the word, and keep your mind on the Lord.

Ex. There is a woman who complains so much that when people see her they know the sky is falling when she begins to speak. She portrays a life of someone that is extremely miserable. Nothing is going right in her life. She refuses to change her speech. Sadly enough she goes to church every Sunday and Wednesday for bible study. She stated that her husband doesn't treat her right, and her family refuses to visit.

She never has one positive thing to say. "She is now sick all the time." If she would change her words, she would change her life.

Sometimes offense may not come from someone else, you can cause your own problems with your mouth and attitude. Having a negative view is a form of offence that hinders your growth and your relationship with God. Make sure that your praise today represents authenticity towards the things of God.

Offence Keeps You From

Enjoying Your Best Life

Praise Day Seven

~ Heart to Heart~

O pen your heart today, and praise from the intimate inner part of your heart. God does not look at the outward appearance of a man; He looks at the heart of a man. The heart of a person always shows itself worthy or unworthy. *1 John 3:20 For if our heart condemn us, God is greater than our heart, and knoweth all things.* Today, know that you are not physically or spiritually able to conceal the inner most parts of your heart.

Your praise should be in truth today. Lay your heart on the altar with the Lord. He will repair the heart if it is broken, lift it higher and reward those who diligently seek Him. Praising God from your heart gives you the encouragement that you need to operate in a supernatural way.

Let's look at David's heart in the book of 1Samuel. David was the youngest of eight children. David was small in stature but exceedingly strong in his heart. His brothers did not respect him, but God favored David. During this time, King Saul needed a champion to fight the Philistine Goliath. Goliath who was a giant and a champion in battle, challenged Israel.

All men feared Goliath, and Goliath who was strong in stature, boasted in pride, that if a man could defeat him, then his people would be Israel's slaves. No one would offer to be a slave if he thought he could be beaten. Goliath was confident in his ability. Goliath didn't consider the ability and favor of God walking with his opponent. If Israel could not produce a champion, then Israel would have to become servants to the Philistines.

Israel was afraid of Goliath. Like many of us, we look at our position and our opponents. If it looks like you are positioned on the weaker team, you may not fight to win because it looks like you are defeated before you start. David had three older brothers who were summoned to fight in the battle to assist Israel. David was commanded by his father to go to the battle field to take his brothers food.

David's brother Eliab's didn't want David there, and told him that he knew his pride the naughtiness of his heart. Eliab's said this to David out of anger. Eliab's assumed that David was there to watch the battle, little did he know that David was there to win the battle. David's heart towards the Lord was pure and innocent.

David, who was not large in stature, was only looked upon as one who should watch the sheep. He was the youngest and no one viewed him as a relevant individual during that time. David had plenty of time on his hands to praise the Lord during the time that he spent watching over the sheep. David acknowledged the Lord in all his ways daily.

God had blessed David to become a mighty warrior during his time watching the sheep. God strengthened him to kill a bear and lion during his time of just watching over the sheep. Because David was obedient to the Lord's voice, he didn't despise the small and unimportant positions that his brothers and others thought he had. Your beginnings are the foundations to your greater position.

David, of course, went on to kill Goliath with a sling and a stone. He hit him in the forehead in the book of 1 Samuel 17. God knew the heart of David, and He strengthened David to do the impossible with what appeared to be a child's toy to win a battle. The world will never understand why you have so much with what appears to be so little in your hands.

When God sees your heart and hears your unconditional and truthful praise towards Him, He will bless you exceedingly and abundantly. *Deuteronomy 10:16 Circumcise therefore the foreskin of your heart, and be no more stiffnecked.* Circumcision removes what does not belong and what is not needed to ensure that you give God a praise that speaks from your heart to his heart.

Imagine yourself with your heart exposed to the Lord. Hand Him your heart and say, Lord I give myself totally to you. I love you Lord, and I want you to know that today my heart is longing only for the things that are pleasing unto you. I decrease so that you increase in my life. You are the only reason I can be or become anything in this world.

Once you understand that the Lord will give you the desires of your heart, why not expose yourself to Him. *Psalm 38:9 Lord, all my desire is before thee; and my groaning is not hid from thee.* Give your praise from your heart. Love on the Lord with the tenacious beat from your heart. Cry out to Him, and tell Him, He is the reason that your heart beats.

He is your first love. Fall in love with Him all over again today. Your heart should be full with all the wonderful and miraculous things that the Lord has done for you. When you think on the things that He is doing and has done for you, your heart should cry out and sing love songs to the Lord. Remember God looks on the inner parts of your heart and soul, not your outer appearance. He knows when you are genuine with your praise.

God Loves You

Praise Day Eight

~ The Refreshing Spirit of God~

Have you ever had a refreshing drink, one that quenched the thirst that felt impossible to quench. Now think about your soul. No one or anything can renew your spirit but God! You can listen to motivational speakers and they can inspire you to push yourself to be successful, but who can refresh your soul and spirit but the Lord. *Romans 15:32 That I may come unto you with joy by the will of God, and may with you be refreshed.*

God desires that you have an encounter with Him that is better than any drink that quenches your thirst. Your praise enters you into His Holy presence. God wants you to experience His love. He desires that everyday is new in Him. He wants to give to you on a daily basis.

45

Your praise connects you to his pleasures. He said that in his presence is fullness of joy. *Psalms 16:11 thou wilt shew me the path of life: in thy presence is fullness of joy: at thy right hand there are pleasures for evermore.* Enter into his presences with praise and thanksgiving.

Speak only the word of God today. Encourage your spirit by reminding yourself of all the blessings that the Lord has bestowed upon you. *Job 32:20, I will speak, that I may be refreshed: I will open my lips and answer.* Today is your day to cogitate on the Lord. Meditating on the word of God is refreshing to your spirit.

Reading the word of God brings revelation knowledge to those who are seeking the Lord. Studying the word indicates to the Lord that you are making Him a priority in your life. Once, God becomes a priority in everything that you are doing, your desires become a priority with God. *1 Corinthians 16:18 For they have refreshed my spirit and yours: therefore acknowledge ye them that are such.*

Once you relish yourself in the word, the will of God becomes embedded in your heart and mind. Refreshing your spirit, allows the Lord strength and power to dwell in you. Growth in the word of God is able to move and instruct you in the things of Christ. It is essential to build your relationship with the Lord.

God gave us the Holy Spirit to assist in your daily walk. In the book of Acts chapter 2 when the Holy Spirit came upon men and they began to speak in other tongues, those who did not understand speaking in tongues thought the men were drunk. Peter interjected and educated the men that no one was drunk but filled with the Spirit of the Lord. *Acts 2:17 And it shall come to pass in the last days, saith God, I will pour out of my Spirit upon all flesh: and your sons and your daughters shall prophesy, and your young men shall see visions, and your old men shall dream dreams.*

Experiencing the refreshing of the Lord is to feel his spirit dwelling on the inside of you. God is not mystical, He is a loving, kind, and forgiving God. *Acts 2:47 Praising God, and having favor with all the people. And the Lord added to the church daily such as should be save.* If God adds to his people daily, He is renewing your spirit and refreshing you on a daily basis. Praise Him to experience his love daily.

Making the effort to experience God's love daily will add to your quality of life. You will find that praising daily will enhance your perception of when the enemy is trying to attack you and his efforts will not prosper. Knowing what is important and being reminded through your praise, keeps you focused on what is truly good for a successful life.

Today, remember it's a new day. You cannot undo yesterday. Start fresh today with a positive view point. Expect

God to do something good for you today. Walk in expectancy every day.

Walk in the Spirit and not your

Flesh

Praise Day Nine

~Renewed~

A renewed spirit is a changed and transformed spirit. Today, praise God for renewing you in the image of Him. *Colossians 3:10 And have put on the new man, which is renewed in knowledge after the image of him that created him.* Change takes time! Think about the metamorphosis that takes place with a worm that changes into a butterfly or a duck that changes into a beautiful swan.

The process of change when it begins may seem daunting, but the finished product is beautiful. God took our old perception of what we thought life should be and renewed us to think in a more profound way. The beauty of God is inside of you. Your will has to allow the cultivation to take place. Once we surrender our will, God's intention for your life will begin to manifest, and the image that is designed specifically for you, will evolve.

Mary was asked to give birth to Jesus. God is such a gentleman that He will never violate your will to live the way you want to live. *Matthew 1:21 And she shall bring forth a son, and thou shalt call his name Jesus: for he shall save his people from their sins.* You have to ask God to come into your life to experience the renewed spirit of God.

When we chose to do our will instead of the will of God, we do not experience the renewed love of God. God said that his people are destroyed for a lack of knowledge. (Hosea 4:6) God will not go against your will if you decide not to live for Him. It is your choice to perish and go to hell.

God is beautiful, merciful, kind, and loving. He built you in the exact image of himself. So when you look in the mirror you have a reason to rejoice about who God really is. He loves you so much that He placed you in the earth to be a representative of Him.

Today, you will speak in a renewed spirit. You will think about how Jesus walked and talked. Think about his loving kindness. *Ephesians 4:23 And be renewed in the spirit of your mind.* Take your mind to the spirit realm. Picture yourself at a table talking with the Lord. Meditating in the word is the key solution with renewing your spirit in the Lord.

Look around the room and take in all the beauty of heaven. Place yourself where the Holy of Holy dwells. God dwells in peace and serenity. Renew your mind to think of

Christ, He is thinking of you. *Jeremiah 29:11 For I know the thoughts that I think toward you, said the Lord, thoughts of peace, and not of evil, to give you an expected end.*

We serve such an awesome God that consistently think about us, and we are constantly on his mind. If we are on his mind, why would you spend your time thinking on things that may keep you from God's best? Today, keep your mind on Him. Praise Him just because He is thinking of you.

Jesus said your name is written in heaven (Luke 10:12). He loves you so much that He has written your name in Heaven. That is a reason to rejoice in the Lord's presence. He loves you! He wants you to know that if you just take the time to renew your spirit and see how blessed you really are, you can enjoy all of the gifts that He has just for you.

Distractions keep you from focusing on the Lord. The enemy wants you to focus on everything but God. He will keep you busy with work, cleaning the house, hanging out with your friends, social networks, and much more. Mary and Martha in the book of Luke 10 is a terrific depiction of not focusing on the Lord's will.

Martha received Jesus in her home for dinner. Mary, who is Martha's sister, was in the home as well. As the evening progressed Jesus began to teach, and Mary chose to sit at the feet of Jesus to listen instead of assisting Martha with cleaning.

Martha became very irritated with Mary not assisting her with cleaning.

Martha petitioned Jesus to tell her sister to come and assist her with cleaning. Jesus who is all knowing did not give in to Martha's request. He did recognize her preoccupation with other things. The Lord preached to Martha letting her know that He will not take away that which is good for Mary.

Mary chose to listen to Jesus. Ask yourself, "Who and what are you choosing to focus on? God wants your undivided attention. During your praise today, clear your mind, and think on how much the Lord loves you. Think about how his grace is surrounding you daily.

When you find yourself thinking of things that are not aligned with the word of God, He requires that you cast down imagination. *1 Chronicles 28:9 And thou, Solomon my son, know thou the God of thy father, and serve him with a perfect heart and with a willing mind: for the Lord searcheth all hearts, and understandeth all the imaginations of the thoughts: if thou seek him, he will be found of thee; but if thou forsake him, he will cast thee off for ever.* In your praise today, keep your mind on God.

When your troubles outweigh your praise, perform the task that normally takes your mind off your troubles. If you like jogging, walking, listening to music, do those things that assist you with clearing your mind. God still accepts your praise because you are willing to give Him praise. He wants you to learn to let go of your problems and praise Him through your process.

You are transparent to God and He wants you to find Him. You can find Him when your heart and mind desires to know Him intimately. Love on Him today with a pure heart. Seek Him and you will find Him.

Example: My son said, "mom I don't believe that everyone at the altar at the church feels the spirit when they are praising God." No, everyone does not feel the spirit, but they understand that praising God even when they don't feel like it, gets God's attention. They understand praise is a weapon. Don't allow your emotions or circumstances to hinder your praise.

Do something different to

Have something different

Take control of Your Mind

Praise Day Ten

~Strengthen Me~

S trength is your praise objective today. Today, thank God for his spiritual strength in your life. God gives us strength to live each day with his grace and mercy. He knows that you will have adversity. He gives you the strength to get through those moments in life that seem unbearable.

Your strength is in the Lord. *2 Samuel 22:33 God is my strength and power, and he maketh my way perfect.* God makes your way perfect if you allow Him in your life. He will take your weakness, faults, tribulations, fears, and turn it around and position you in the winner's circle. He never wants you to feel defeated. You have to want and believe that his power will strengthen you.

Let's look at Moses. Moses had an incredible responsibility of having to go to Pharaoh and tell Him to free the people of Israel. When God first spoke to Moses, he did not want the task to lead the people. Moses actually ran away when God had instructed Him to lead the people after a chain of events.

Although he ran away, he submitted himself, and returned to do what God instructed him to do when he first asked. God had to strengthen Moses to become the leader that He had created him to be. There will be times in your life that you will have to do things that you don't feel that you are strong enough or qualified enough to do. This is the moment that you run to the Lord instead of running from your destiny.

What ever it is that you are running from, you will have to eventually face your fears. If you are a father or mother who neglected your responsibilities, you will eventually have to face those children that you neglected. If you ran away from your spouse, family, or life, you will have to face what you are running from. You don't have to run away, just ask God to strengthen you to handle your obligations or fears.

Psalms 28:8 The Lord is their strength, and he is the saving strength of his anointed. Moses was God's anointed and so are you. He has anointed each of us with different gifts. We have to trust that God knows your fears and He will give you the strength to complete your task.

When Jesus knew that his time was near to carry the cross. He prayed to God and asked him to remove this cup from him. Although, he did not want to go through the persecution of the world, He knew that if He did not complete his task, our sins would not be forgiven. God strengthened Jesus to do His will. God will strengthen you if you ask. God is not a respecter of persons.

He does not have a favorite person. He loves you the same as He loves the man next to you. He has unconditional love for you. So why not thank Him for the strength that He has provided for you on a daily basis.

He loves renewing your spirit. God loves you. He will not keep any good thing away from you. Why not praise a God that loves you more than you can even comprehend. *Psalm 62:7 In God is my salvation and my glory: the rock of my strength, and my refuge, is in God.* When you realize that you are safe in the God that you serve, you should run to do his will.

If you understand that the God that you serve is your foundation, why not trust in God. He wants you to rely on Him for everything in your life. When you are able to persevere in the midst of adversity and still know that God will provide you with strength that you need, why not praise Him. *Isaiah 40:29 He giveth power to the faint; and to them that have no might he increaseth strength.* God wants to strengthen you to defeat the storms when they come or when you become distracted with life's experiences, so that you will not drown in your adversity. God wants your praise daily. He wants you to pull from Him. He wants to strengthen you in his strength. He wants to pour out His spirit in you. You have to receive what God wants for you. Receive His strength through your praise.

Learn a new scripture today.

Praise Day Eleven

~ Forgive~

W alking in forgiveness of past and present disappointments may seem to be a daunting way to live. Forgiving people who have hurt you seem impossible. Jesus stated how often we are to forgive those who hurt us. Seventy times seven times per day is how often you are to forgive those who cause pain, disappointment, and destruction.

Praising God when you have unforgiveness in your heart hinders your praise. *In Mark 11:25 And when ye stand praying forgive if ye have ought against any: that your Father also which is in heaven may forgive you your trespasses.* If unforgiveness hinders your prayers, it also hinders your praise, and growth, in the Lord. How can one truly walk in love, if you have bitterness, and resentment in your heart?

Exercising your faith is instrumental with forgiving someone. *Hebrews 11:1 Now Faith is the substance of things hoped for, the evidence of things not seen.* God is looking at your heart, mind, and soul. You want to stand before Him with a clean heart. Forgive those who have hurt you even if they never ask for forgiveness.

You are special and divinely created. God loves hearing from you. Your joy is the Lord. Trust Him to remove the pain and sorrow. It may not happen over night, but just know that if you would just fast forward a year from today, and think on where you want to be, it would not include the pain and anguish in your life today. Change your thinking, to change your outcome. You deserve to walk in the love and the grace of God.

Praising God when you have unforgiveness in your heart hinders you praise. If unforgiveness hinders your prayers, it also hinders your growth in the Lord. How can one truly walk in love if you have bitterness and resentment in your heart?

You want God's best in your life. You want to feel the presence of Him all day long. The closeness that comes with praise should not be hindered because of anger, strife, and resentment. Let's look at it this way. An ideal credit score is 860.

With an 860 you can purchase anything you want. Your credit score states that you are trustworthy, reliable, dependable, and creditable.

Credit score dictates your interest rate when purchasing a house or a car. What if God looked at your unforgiveness as a credit score. We often want God to forgive us of our indiscretions but we are not as lenient on those who caused us harm. Look at the wicked servant who would not forgive those who were indebted to him, but he asked for forgiveness from his master who did forgive him of his debt in Matthew 18:32.

This man judged those harshly who owed him money. Once his master was informed of his servant's wickedness, he then cast the yoke around his neck. God is a just God. Keep your heart clean with forgiveness. It may not be the easiest task, but it is truly the one worth practicing to walk in the presence of God.

The Bible states that it is okay to get angry but sin not. People are emotional beings. You will have days when everyone is annoying, but you have to find that space that belongs to just you and God and enter in with praise. There is always a moment to just stop yourself and ask yourself, is this problem really worth hindering my growth in the admonition of the Lord?

Sometimes walking away is better than standing to argue, fight, and speak things in the atmosphere that you will regret and have to repent later. My son was 9 years old when he repeated what another 9 year old said to him. The little boy told him he had nothing, no friend, home, and those words of degradation offended me. I got so angry that a child had spoken to my son in that manner.

Before I knew it, my voice changed negatively, and I put my hands on my hips, and said "what did you say back to him?" I was silently hoping he had told him off, and as I waited for a hastily response, which did not come as quickly as I had hoped because he was eating an apple. As I watched him chew each bite of his apple, he finally said, oh, "I told him his words meant nothing, and he should not have taken the time to speak them in the atmosphere, because those words fell down to the ground."

Instead of getting angry or even with his accuser, he treated him as Jesus would have. The child taught me, what I had been teaching him. He was the bigger person. I had to ask for forgiveness just that quickly. My son forgave and went on to play without any hesitation. God wants you and I to forgive quickly before we have the chance to harbor ill will in our hearts.

I understand that life situations may have caused you to be offended with those who may have robbed, raped, beat, or mistreated you. God is a restorer of all things. Forgive those who have trespassed against you. The kingdom of God is at hand, and nothing or no one should prevent you from entering in the kingdom that is rightfully yours to have.

Praise God today for allowing you to walk in forgiveness. Stay in the presence of God to receive all that He has for you. He wants your soul to prosper.

Pray for those who hurt you

Praise Day Twelve

~ Satisfied Praise~

In today's society, you must be technology savvy or you will be left behind in the dark ages if you haven't upgraded your phones, televisions, and computers. Our society is very fast paced, and this leaves most people vicariously with an unsatisfied flesh. This may spill over in your praise life.

It is easy to misconstrue satisfaction with being satisfied. Take the time to look at a child who is throwing a tantrum in public, and the parent who is embarrassed by the behavior. Parents often attempt to stop the negative behavior with rewarding the child with the satisfaction of getting their way. This works for that moment, but the child will continue the behavior again because true satisfaction did not occur when the child received what he or she thought they needed.

Throwing a tantrum is a form of manipulation for a child to control the parent. Getting the object at that time isn't really what will satisfy the child, only controlling the parent. The same behavior is shown in praise.

This behavior lingers into your praise life. Single people complain about being single, married people complain about being married, poor people complain about poverty, and who knows what the rich complain about. When praising God those individuals are focused on what they think will make them complete. People often praise God with a purpose of what they think they need instead of praising with the purpose of uplifting God. Instead, they offer God what appears to be a praise of satisfaction for themselves. Not realizing it is a praise of selfishness.

Praise is established to please God, not to satisfy your wants. When you become systematic with your praise, you lose the authenticity of the praise. When you praise to get a return on your investment, you are not authentic. You are only praising for the satisfaction of the return. Ask yourself is God satisfied with that type of praise. Earlier I gave you an example of how God stretched 100 dollars. Was that a selfish praise, or an authentic praise?

That praise was authentic. I praised God for what I had, and I believed that what I had, would be enough to take care of my needs. I didn't ask God for more, just to bless what I had. Don't get me wrong, there isn't anything wrong with asking God for anything. He wants you to ask Him, but He wants you to not be selfish with what you are asking.

Offering God a satisfied praise regardless of what you are going through speaks to the trust that you have for the Lord. When you are in a satisfied state, you are trusting God with your life. A satisfied praise says to God that you understand that He is in control and you are totally dependent upon Him. In *Ezekiel 16:28 Thou hast played the whore also with the Assyrians, because thou wast unsatiable; yea, thou hast played the harlot with them, and yet couldest not be satisfied.* The word unsatiable means not satisfied in the strong concordance.

In Ezekiel, this scripture is depicting an unsatisfied spirit. When someone is not satisfied the behavior that is exuded reflects instability, unfocused, not reliable, and selfishness. An unsatisfied spirit blames God for unanswered prayers and often does not acknowledge God for the good in their lives. Those individuals believe that they have goodness in their lives, because they produced it on their own. That is self satisfaction. When you understand that God is the satisfier, your spirit will praise Him for His presence in your daily life.

Your satisfaction comes from God and not man, God is your satisfier. God will give you a return on your investment for your praise once you understand that it is not what you think He should do.

Be Authentic with Your Praise

Praise Day Thirteen

~ Praise for Your Children~

A sk a woman who has had a child or one that had the opportunity to take care of a child as her own, she will tell you that children are gifts from God. They are more than just amusement. They are individuals who need guidance and instructions to become successful in life. The Bible speaks of two women, Hannah and Sarah who desired to have children.

Hannah petitioned God until He answered her. She offered the unborn child to Him. You know you are offering God a radical praise when you negotiate something or someone that you don't have in your possession in the physical. Sarah had a husband who was obedient to the Lord, and He restored her womb to make the vision and promise come to pass concerning a child.

Both parents, Hannah and Sarah, understood that the child belonged to God. God honored his promise to bless them with children and in return the parents honored the agreement and gave God the child they blessed them with. When you have children, those children are only your children for a season. When you offer your child up to God, you are telling Him, I trust you to take care of this child.

If you offered your child to God and your child ended up in prison, on drugs and alcohol, or just living a life that you know that God did not plan for them to endure, remember we are free moral agents, your children will make decisions that you may not always agree with, but if you just trust and believe the Lord, He will always come to your defense. *Psalms 27:14 KJV Wait on the Lord: be of good courage, and he shall strengthen thine heart; wait I say, on the Lord.*

God did not stop delivering children just because they were in prison. The walls that the enemy has placed surrounding your child does not prevent a loving God from penetrating the most astute wall. He didn't stop delivering children just because they made a conscious decision to use drugs and alcohol. Understand that some visions tarry. But wait, God always comes through. *Psalms 130:5 KJV I wait for the Lord, my soul doth wait, and in his word do I hope.*

Remind God of his words that He has promised you. If you did not offer up your child during birth, don't worry, the altar didn't move. Place all your trust in Him to deliver your child. Praise God for the unseen as Hannah did. Hannah's son strayed away from God's word. He was chained and his eyes were plucked out of his sockets.

When Samuel came to himself, he remembered to call on the Lord. God redeemed Samuel. God restored him back to his natural glory before he died. God always get the victory. Will you praise God for the victory before you see it? Will you give Him your heart and trust that He always keeps his word? *Matthew 24:35 Heaven and earth will pass away but my words shall not pass away..*

We often hear the scripture Proverbs 22:6 KJV *Train up a child in the way he should go: and when he is old, he will not depart from it.* It is vital that you truly understand what this scripture means. The context is always taken out of content when children are not going in the right direction.

The spirit of the Lord wants you to evaluate if you gave your child Church or if you are giving your child God. Proverbs 22:6 means for you to train your child in the things of Christ. If you took your child to church, but Monday through Saturday, they saw you cursing, committing adultery, drinking, doing drugs, and going to the clubs on Saturday, but on Sunday, you put on your Sunday best and go to church, you have given your kids church and not God.

Don't worry if you did, remember the altar has not moved. There is time to correct the problem. I was vicariously listening to a conversation that was misguided in the concept of training up a child. The women who were speaking said, don't worry about your kids, you took them to church on Sunday, they will come back to what they know.

What is it that they know exactly? How can a child come to a God that they don't know. They will only show up in church on Sunday and continue to do what you did Monday through Saturday, because that is what you trained them to do. There are a few children who deviate from the norm because they made a decision not to be like you. Those children will serve God!

Now that you have a clear understanding of what you may or may not have done with your child, don't worry. The altar has not moved. Repent and place your petitions before the Lord concerning your child. Praise God for the positive outcome for your children. Believe that God is the redeemer who sits high and looks low. He said that He knew you before you were formed. Will you trust God to undo your mistakes when you were blind and could not see?

Praise God for the favor that He has placed upon your head and your children's head. Never give up on the hope of God. On my mother's death bed she looked up at her young daughter and said, "I'm not worried about you, I have given you to God, you and your sister will be fine." It's something powerful when you know that even in death God will still deliver your children. Praise God, trust God, and give your child to Him.

Don't give up on Family

Praise Day Fourteen

~ Dance Praise~

Rejoicing before the Lord is a gesture that is looked upon as favorable in the Lord's eyes. Singing and dancing is a form of praise, and it ushers the Lord into your presence. Your praise connects you to the Lord's power, and you get to enjoy the overflow of your praise.

Remember when David praised that he danced out of his clothes in 2 Samuel 6:14. David feared the Lord, he had seen how God smote Uzzah for his error. In 2Samuel 6 this book teaches several lessons.

1. Desire to praise

2. Repercussions from offensive spirits

3. Blessing from a praising spirit

David had 30,000 men to bring the ark of God from the house of Abinadab. The ark was so special that David and all the house of Israel played music with various instruments before the Lord. Uzzah for reasons placed his hand to the Ark. God was not pleased and he died the very moment that he committed this act of disobedience.

David witnessed what the Lord had done and fear was place in his heart. David was so afraid of the Ark that he left the ark in another city for three months. The city was blessed, and he knew of the blessings that God had given that city. David's spirit was rekindled and he had the people to go back to the city and retrieve the Ark of God.

David was so happy just knowing that God was going to bless Him and the people, that he danced out of his linen e`phod, which is a vest that high priest wore. This garment was held in high regards among the people, just as a King and Queen who wear crowns. David understood that praise comes before, during, and after you have your results.

Why wait to praise God after you see your manifestation? Praise Him before you see it. This builds the foundation of trust between you and God. David did get discouraged, when he left the ark of God in another city, but he regrouped and praised God again.

Staying focused during the time that you don't see the promise coming to pass, is a crucial moment. You have to stay focused, although the vision may tarry, just continue to believe that the Lord has not forgotten you, and He is working on your behalf to bring your vision to pass. He loves you more than you can even conceptualize.

Michal, the daughter of Saul, saw David dancing and she became very offended. She told him that he did not represent himself well by dancing and taking off his clothes in front of the help. She told him that he shamelessly uncovered himself. Isn't that how people react when they don't understand your praise? When they may know or have been privy to see your shameful experiences?

Be careful not to judge why someone else is praising God. You don't know what they are going through, or what they may have been through, and they are still standing. Michal, needless to say, never had a child. Never judge someone else's praise, experienced the Lord for yourself!

Today, praise God with your dance, music, and song. Don't ever be ashamed of praising God. He wants you to know that He loves you. When you praise Him your spirit becomes closer to Him. You are expressing your joy for the Lord.

It doesn't matter what others perceive of your praise. If David actually cared about what others thought, he would have missed the opportunity to be an example to others. Regardless, of who you are, and what you have, you are never big enough, important enough, not to give God praise. He is God, and He deserves your uninterrupted attention.

Praise God today, as if today is the last day that you have to praise Him. Give Him a praise that exceeds your previous praise. Love on Him today with all of your heart. He loves you and want only the best for you.

Enjoy Your Blessings

Praise Day Fifteen

~ God Has Birth A Blessing Inside of You~

The blessing inside of you can and will be unleashed with your praise. Praise stirs up the hunger for the Lord inside of you. Some people live their entire lives not knowing what their gifts are. You have to come before God and ask Him what gifts are lying dormant inside of you.

Birthing a child into the world is a special, but cumbersome experience. At the onset of the conception and the realization that a child is inside of you, everything changes about the outcome of your life. When a baby begins to grow inside a woman's body, she changes on the inside and outside her attitude, eating habits, and she takes on a new form.

This transition takes place inside of every individual who becomes aware of the gift that has been placed inside of them just waiting to become a reality. God transforms you from the inside out. Although, you are aware that you have this gift, it doesn't show up immediately, just like the child.

God has to work on you from the inside first. A woman's body has to expand to make room for the child that is growing. A body builder has to change his eating along with working out to see the desired outcome. God will change you, to ensure that you are able to use all the resources needed to be successful. Your gift will make room for you. Meaning, if you need to go to school to make your dream a reality, God will make a way so that you can start the process to walk out your gift. Your gift may be waiting at the end of a two, four, or six year education plan.

Your gift has to be nurtured with the ingredients to become successful before you give birth to it. Just as a child takes nine months before entering the world, your gift may take time also. Don't rush the process, nor despise the process. Make sure you are learning how to walk in your gift from a Godly perspective. You always want to please God in everything that you do.

If you praise and ask God to show you your gifts, He will do just that. Once the Lord gives you a preview of your life it is up to you to run your race. Remember Him as you walk in your gift. Remember Him always in your gifts. *Deuteronomy 4:9 Only take heed to thyself, and keep thy soul diligently, lest thou forget the things which thine eyes have seen, and lest they depart from thy heart all the days of thy life: but teach them thy sons, and thy sons' sons.*

God is reminding you that whatever you do, don't forget Him, and don't forget how you received your gift. God blessed you to be a blessing. You are responsible for assisting and showing others the way. Your gifts are not just for you, but you are an instrument that belongs to God.

You are his representation in the earth. You are responsible for teaching others to praise God. You are responsible for teaching your children and your children's children how to praise and trust the Lord.

Teach them how to access all of the gifts that are inside of them and how to constantly praise the Lord. Remember to give back to God. Honor Him and acknowledge Him in all your ways.

God is not a respecter of persons. *Acts 10:34 then Peter opened his mouth, and said, Of a truth I perceive that God is no respecter of persons.* Never be jealous or envious of another person's gift. We all have different gifts. You can praise God and thank Him for what He has birthed inside of you. When God places a seed inside of you, you have to water that seed. You have to research, work, and cultivate the seed that has been placed inside of you. If you do nothing, how can you birth the very thing that God has placed inside of you?

Today, praise God for the gift that is inside of you. Your foundation is stable with God. Continue to praise Him to build upon your foundation. *Luke 6:48 He is like a man which built an house, and dig deep, and laid the foundation on a rock: and when the flood arose, the steam beat vehemently upon that house, and could not shake it: for it was founded upon a rock.*

Your foundation is strong. Continue to praise God. Don't get discouraged with anything that comes your way. Remember who you belong to, remember who is blessing you, and remember He knew you in the womb, so He has great things just for you. Don't forget God, praise Him every day. God loves you! Walk in your gift. A very good friend once said, "settle it in your mind," you are a champion.

Your Dreams Are Meant to

Come True

Praise Days Sixteen

~ Frustrated Purpose~

The book of Ezra is such a profound learning experience for those of you who know what your gifts are, and your purpose has been frustrated with distractions that are beyond your control. Remember there is a spiritual realm where the angels in heaven are working diligently to get you to your destinations.

When you praise you are speaking not only in the earthly realm but the spiritual realm. That is why it is vitally important for you to speak even in your frustrations only the word of God. *In Matthew 16:19 And I will give unto thee the keys of the kingdom of heaven: and whatsoever thou shalt bind on earth shall be bound in heaven: and whatsoever thou shalt loose on earth shall be loosed in heaven.*

Your words shape, transform, and produce the exact environment you desire. So speak life in every word that you speak. It really is a matter of life and death. Praise God and rebuke anything that may hinder your growth. There is a real enemy that does not want you to be successful and who wants you to give up on God. You are too close to give up now. Persevere to produce whole life prosperity.

Picture yourself setting your goals, working towards those goals, and sadly, life happens and your plans are altered for a season. You may have wanted to go to school, start a business, or just move from one location to the next. Regardless of what you may have desired to do, or if God showed you what He needed for you to do. Once you have the premonition to do something, there are forces in the earth to deter you from achieving your goal.

In Ezra 4:5 part of the text says, *And hired counselors against them, to frustrate their purpose,* all the days of Cyrus King of Persia, even until the reign of Darius King of Persia. Ask yourself, "What are the obstacles that are frustrating your purpose?" In the book of Ezra the people of God wanted to build a temple unto the Lord God of Israel.

Each time the people attempted to build the temple, they were distracted with those who stopped their performance with ridiculous pay toll, tributes and custom. The people persevered, although their purpose was purposely frustrated. You have to examine the intentions of those who say they are trying to help but only hinder. They may only want to frustrate your purpose.

During this time, the people offered praises up to the Lord daily. Remember even in the midst of your frustration that you have to praise. Never stop giving God praise and thanksgiving. Your praise moves you closer to your destination. *Ezra 3:11 And they sang together by course in praising and giving thanks unto the Lord: because he is good, for his mercy endureth for ever toward Israel. And all the people shouted with a great shout, when they praised the Lord, because the foundation of the house of the Lord was laid.*

How strong is your foundation? Make sure that you are grounded in your word to fight any obstacles with the word of God. Always search the Bible for a solution concerning your problem. Only God can and will give you your heart's desire.

I encourage you to praise God for those who come to frustrate your purpose. They are instrumental in your testimony. They are the people who keep you in prayer and praise. Praying for those who come only to destroy your

destiny, also indicates to God that you are maturing in the word of God. Your focus isn't the individual or the circumstance, your focus is on God. Keep your mind on Him. During your frustration, you spend that time consulting and trusting God. Don't allow a frustrated purpose to hinder your destiny.

Your work will be remembered

Praise Day 17

~ Praising Through Fear~

***

Fear is the one characteristic, which enables an individual from maximizing their potential. Fear aborts, annihilate, criticizes, cheats, lies, and hinders the work of God flowing in the believer's life. When you think of fear, it is realistic to think of natural tangible objects or innate things when you think of fear.

What about fear that keeps you from being successful? Draw an imaginary line in front of you. On the opposite side are your dreams and aspirations. On the side that you are standing on, are all the reasons that you have placed in front of the line to keep you from going to the other side.

One of the most popular stories in the bible which is taught from thousands of pulpits, is the story of Peter and Jesus walking on water. (Matthew 14:28) Peter asked Jesus could he come out on the water to walk with Him. Jesus said yes, and once Peter started walking, he looked at the water instead of keeping his eyes on Jesus. Most individuals look at their circumstances. The waves distracted him and he began to sink. Peter understood that he needed to call on Jesus in the midst of his circumstances, you must remember to keep your focus on Jesus.

Peter's experience is a wonderful depiction of fear and rescue in the Bible. Let's look at the woman who was fearful that her two sons would become slaves to clear a debt that the father owed. This woman was desperate, and needed a solution to save her sons from a life of slavery. She went to the prophet for guidance, and he asked her what did she have in her house?

She said, "a pot of oil." He instructed her to borrow vessels and fill each with the oil to sell and pay the debt. This woman obeyed and she prevented the sale of her sons into the debtor's hands. She had a fear of her children being taken away which encouraged her to do something different to prevent a negative outcome.

Fear paralyzes the growth of the believer to reach their potential in life. Fear comes in many forms that allow individuals to stay in a stagnated state. Praise builds the confidence in the believer to achieve the impossible. Once you understand how praise not only edifies God, praise also gives you the inner strength to move forward regardless of circumstances.

Transformation from fear to freedom is your goal. Fear is real, but it is not of God. *1 John 4:4 Ye are of God, little children, and have overcome them: because greater is he that is in you, than he that is in the world.* God sees you as an overcomer. There isn't anything that you are not capable of achieving. He gave you the Holy Spirit that dwells in you to strengthen, encourage, and bless you.

When you truly know who you are, and whom dwells within you, you begin to understand what you have access to. You are equipped with unlimited amount of grace, favor, and the power of God. Allow your praise daily to speak to the Lord. Thank Him for removing the fear that hinders you. Praise Him for giving you more of Him, and to walk in his love and grace.

You have the innate ability to change your circumstances whenever you want. Open your mouth and let the power of your praise bring the change that you so desire in your life. Making God your priority daily increases your access to a more fulfilling life.

Praising God daily gives you access to his ear. Children have the desire to be heard by their parents. They will do anything to get their attention, even if it means throwing a tantrum in the middle of the floor. Praise gives you direct access to your father.

Psalm 4:1 Hear me when I call O God of my righteousness: thou has enlarged me when I was in distress: have mercy upon me, and hear my prayer. Praising God when you are in distress with fear speaks to Him.

Don't take for granted that your voice is not important. You have the power in your mouth to transform your life in a greater way. Access your power today with your praise. Unleash the power and the ability that God has given you. *Psalm 4:7 Thou hast put gladness in my heart, more than in the time that their corn and their wine increase.*

It should be your desire to put gladness in the heart of the Lord with your praise. God wants you to spend time with Him although He increases you, He doesn't want you to be distracted with things, but to stay focused on Him. Give God the praise and you will not dwell on fear, lack, anger, or anything that takes you away from God. You will increase daily in knowledge, and you will walk in the confidence that God hears you!

Be of Good Courage

Praise Day Eighteen

~Walk With God~

Walking with God does not require your sight, but it requires your spirit. Helen Keller, a woman who was blind and deaf, understood love without the very tangible senses of sight and hearing. Many of us need to see and hear the word of God to conceptualize God.

Helen Keller stated, "Love can't be seen or even touched, it must be felt with the heart." She understood that her heart is the key to her success. God is a Spirit, you have to make a supernatural connection with your mind, spirit, and body to connect to Him.

As I stated in the first chapter, you have to remove your intellect to understand God. Your walk has to be extraordinary. To become extraordinary in your walk, you have to let go of your

97

belief of who God is, and allow God to show you who He is. This requires trust and belief in the word of God.

Your walk with God depends on how willing you are to let go of yourself. Your praise connects you to Him. God will bring to your remembrance his power and ability in your life. If you take the time to think about how you were delivered from tribulation, or when you were strengthened to complete your goals, and when you cheated death on countless occasions.

You were only able to achieve the testimony because of God! Praise is a spiritual connection. You don't have to be perfect to walk with God. Everyone makes mistakes, and God knew that you would make mistakes. You were saved by grace.

Your walk with God is not meant for God to understand you, but for you to understand God. Don't place Him in a bottle as if he is a Genie, and will appear only when you are desolate or in trouble. He is almighty, and He is with you all the time. You are never alone.

Your praise daily strengthens your ability mentally and spiritually that God is with you. *1 Thessalonians 4:1 Furthermore then we beseech you, brethren, and exhort you by the Lord Jesus, that as ye have received of us how ye ought to walk and to please God, so ye would abound more and more.* Abounding more and more is to increase greatly of good things.

Praising God pleases Him, and pleasing God increases your knowledge of wisdom, grace, and favor because you are seeking Him. People will look at you and see the light of God flowing through you. God gives you free gifts of grace. (Romans 5:15)

Job is a man who Satan afflicted destruction in his life. Satan asked God could he afflict tribulation upon Job. Job walked with God and Satan desperately wanted to prove that in the midst of loss, destruction, and tribulation that even Job would walk away from God.

Job had moments of despair, and those around him felt that he must have done something so horrible in the eyes of God, that God cursed him. God will never curse the people that He created. There are generational curses that people inherit or you may curse yourself with sin. However, God himself rebukes the curse so that you and your children do not inherit that curse once you give your life to Him.

He blessed you with grace. It would be a contradiction of the word for Him to curse you. At the end of the story, Job was given back all the things he lost and he abound more and more exceeding greater than he had before Satan came to destroy him.

Your walk with God should never be contingent upon the good times. You have to understand that your praise walk should be just as strong when you are happy as well as challenged. Praising God keeps you connected to your healer, miracle worker, your sustainer, your way maker, and your forgiver. God keeps you daily.

Praise God to stay connected to Him. Praise God to strengthen your walk with Him. Praise allows you to hear the Lord speaking to you. You will know his voice.

During my first years as a new believer, I had an issue going on in my life that I needed to get clarification on how to handle that problem. I had an engaging conversation with my sister in Christ, which happens to be my hair stylist.

She said, "give me three days, and I will get back with you." I said what is going to happen in three days. She said, "I am going to fast and praise God to get a word from Him."

She spoke of Him as if she was getting ready to call Him. At that moment, I wanted the same relationship with God. He is not a respecter of persons, so what was hindering me from hearing from God.

I was hindering the voice of God by not Praising, praying, and fasting. I got connected to hear from God on my own. Our relationship is strong, because I desired to hear from Him.

I know his voice. I hear Him and build on my relationship daily because of Praise. Increase your praise and strengthen your walk with the Lord.

You should desire to walk and hear from God daily. Bless the Lord today, seek Him and you will have Him. Walk with Him by communicating with Him daily. Praise Him, He is Enough!

He is Enough!

In Him, He has equipped you with enough to be everything you desire to become, and everything He needed you to be in Him, you're enough!

In Him you have enough to move forward, succeed in life, climb mountains, run obstacles, laugh at adversity, grab your future by the horns, because IN Him you have enough.

You're not promised a life without tribulation, but you are promised that He will give you the beauty for your ashes. He is enough!

Your praise is a weapon, it tears down depression, kills negativity, uplifts God, renews your spirit, transforms your thinking, encourages the broken hearted, feeds the poor. He is enough!

Give God the Praise today forgiving your sins, opening the doors of opportunity, not remembering your past, changing your present, and moving you into your successful future. God is Enough!

God is Everything that You

Need

Praise Day Nineteen

~ Weeping ~

W hen a child is weeping the parent often goes to the aid of the child to try to understand the problem and determine a solution to the problem. God performs the same miracle in the believer's life. *Psalm 126:5-6 They that sow in tears shall reap in joy. He that goeth forth and weepeth, bearing precious seed, shall doubtless come again with rejoicing, bringing his sheaves with him.*

Weeping to the Lord will get his attention, but know that He knows the difference in your weeping. God will not be manipulated with false tears. He said that the weeping has to be precious seed, meaning you have to be sincere with your weeping. There are several types of weeping:

a. Manipulative weeping

b. Grieving weeping

c. Rescue weeping

d. Praising weeping

Manipulative weeping is a selfish weeping. Manipulative weeping only wants the attention of others to feel sorry for them. One weeps long and hard to make God move on their behalf. When that individual does not receive the expected outcome from God, then God is blamed for not delivering on the promise.

This individual is an attention seeker, cries easily when others are around, and constantly seeks reassurance. Manipulative weeping is for others and not sincere from the heart. God sees you and He knows your heart. He will not be bullied into blessing you because you are throwing a tantrum. If this is you, spend real time with the Lord and give Him a real praise.

Grieving weeping is the weeping that occurs during the loss of a love one, job, or relationship. Grieving may also be caused by distress, anger, or anything that has caused pain in your life. In Genesis 29 there is a story of Jacob, Rachel, and Leah. Leah was given to Jacob who never wanted her.

She was hated, and she grieved tremendously. God saw that she was hated and He blessed her by opening up her womb. Instead of embracing the blessing, in her despair she gave her first three children names after the pain, resentment, and despair that afflicted her. Leah's fourth child was named Judah because she realized in the midst of her pain, she needed to praise the Lord.

Leah's weeping was noticed and she did not have a hidden agenda to manipulate the Lord. He blessed her because out of her weeping was a precious seed. She was sincere and her heart cried out to God. Let your praise be one of authenticity.

Rescue weeping occurs when you want God to bring you out of your troubles. You don't want to go through the trouble, pain, or destruction. You are calling on God to come in the midst of your adversity and save you from your problems. *Psalms 35:17-18 Lord, how long wilt thou look on? Recue my soul from their destructions, my darling from the lions. v18, I will give thee thanks in the great congregation: I will praise thee among much people.*

When rescue praise occurs, one wants to make an exchange with God. You promise to give Him Praise if He delivers you from your adversity. You will tell everyone that it was God and not you. God sees and knows all. When people have been afflicted by others, know that God saw them when they did it! Nothing is a surprise to God but it is always a surprise to the person who is going through the affliction.

God will deliver you from your affliction, and it may not be the way you want the deliverance to come. Treat your rescue praise as a learning experience. Thank God for removing the adversity before it happens and forgive in the midst of your adversity. Forgiveness is always necessary when you are standing before the Lord.

Lastly, a weeping praise! *Luke 7:44 And he turned to the woman, and said unto Simon, Seest thou this woman: I entered into thine house, thou gavest me no water for my feet: but she hath washed my feet with tears, and wiped them with the hairs of her head.* This woman praised Jesus with her tears.

She gave Him a just because praise. She loved on Jesus because of who He is and not because of anything that He had given her. He did bless her, but what is poignant about the story, she praised Him with her tears without asking for anything. Will you praise Him for the things that He has blessed you with. Give God a praise because of who He is.

Remind Him of who He is to you and how you appreciate the love that He has bestowed upon you and your family. You have a reason to praise Him, dig deep inside of yourself and just think about how good He is to you. Your soul has a reason to give God the praise.

Give thanks to the Lord because He is good!

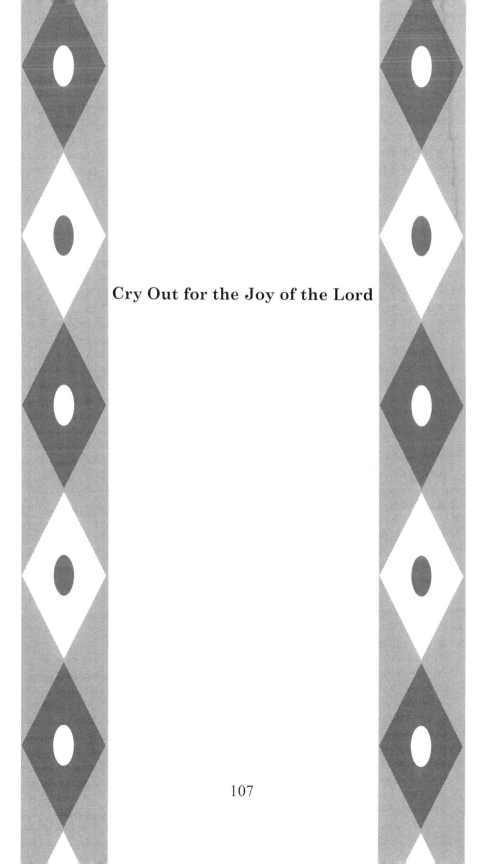

Cry Out for the Joy of the Lord

Praise Day 20

~ Hidden Treasure ~

Treasures are the items, people, or places that are seen as symbolic, influence, or precious in value to the individual. Treasures are protected by you to ensure that the value does not depreciate. People that we value, we take care of and never hurt. The items that are precious are kept safe to protect them from damage or theft. God's word is a hidden treasure that needs to be searched and embedded in your heart.

Proverbs 2:3-5, Yea, if thou criest after knowledge, and liftest up thy voice for understand; 4.If thou sleekest her as silver, and searchest for her as for hid treasures; 5.Then shalt thou understand the fear of the Lord, and find the knowledge of God. God wants you to desperately seek his word to understand who He is, trust in Him, and allow his word to transform your life. When you have a greater understanding of who God is, you will have a better understanding of the will for your life.

How can you truly understand what his will for your life is, if you have not sought his word to understand who He is. If you seek Him, you will find Him. Do not take reading the word of God for granted. In his word, He answers all of your questions. You never have to worry about Him wavering in what He is saying to you.

God is not like your friends and family. He gives you the right words all the time and He is not emotional or hold grudges when you share your emotions with Him. You can rely on Him to direct you in everything that you do. If you don't hear Him, Get in your quiet place to read and allow the word of God to grow inside of you. *Deuteronomy 28:12 The Lord shall open unto thee his good treasure, the heaven to give the rain unto thy land in his season, and to bless all the work of thine hand.*

Do you hear what the Lord is saying to you in that scripture? He will open unto you his good treasure. He loves you, and today if you will start spending time with Him reading his word and praising Him, He will rain upon you in this season. God will give you the ability and strength to walk in your gift. You may be in the valley of decision concerning starting your own business, changing jobs, moving to a new city, or making a life change to get married or divorce. Whatever it is that you need wisdom to do, you will find it in the word of God.

God wants you to search for Him today, and everyday. He desires that you unlock the mysteries of life, with understanding your purpose in life through his word. Rain represents the blessing poured out upon you. So every time it rains, you should rejoice. Today, your praise should reflect not only the treasures that God has given you, but also for the blessing of the rain. This is your season, and God wants you to have everything that He has designed just for you.

He is a very loving father who wants to protect you in the midst of adversity, but He is the same God who wants you to apply the word in your life. He wants you to walk in divine whole life prosperity. He wants you to prosper in you love walk, health and wellness, economically, and physically. He wants you to understand that when you seek the hidden treasures in the word, you desire to love Him as much as He loves you.

Have you ever searched for your keys or your cell phone? You know that panic feeling that you have when you can't find your keys and cell phone. You literally tear the house down, and re-track every step you made to find your items. Before you know it, you have become so frustrated that you cry out to God and ask Him to help you find those items you feel that you cannot make it through the day without.

That is how you should search the word of God, with the same tenaciousness that your day will not be fruitful without Him. Your keys keep you from moving, your phone keeps you from communicating, but without the word, you cannot move nor communicate successfully without guidance. Seek the treasures that God has for you in his word. Let the word of God bless you.

Today, Praise God by starting off with, Heavenly Father, I seek your treasures that you have for me today. I have an ear to hear, eyes to see, and a heart that is ready to receive. I need for you to speak to me concerning your will for me. I want a clear understanding of how you want to change me from inside out. I'm yours Lord, and my only desire is to do your will in Jesus name.

Today God, I want to partner with you to see beyond my natural eyes. I want to take a glimpse in the spiritual realm to see past my emotions. I realize I know absolutely nothing without you. I will walk where you say walk, I will do what you say to do. God, I am seeking your treasures today and everyday!

Everything you need is

Inside of You

Praise Day Twenty One

~ It's All About Him~

D r. R.A. Vernon preached a sermon called, "It's All About Him!" Dr. R.A. Vernon's sermon reminded me of how we can sometimes start our day thinking about ourselves instead of God. Today, if you started your day off with jumping out the bed, running to the shower, or turning on the TV, you just indicated that you are not putting God first. You are guiding your day and not the Lord. You are walking in your own will and not his. When you start your day off with spending time with God first, then you understand that it is ALL ABOUT HIM!

Jesus, Jesus, Jesus, it's all about you. Your praise is not for you. Your praise is for Him. He is using you to be an instrument in the earth to bring his people to Him. You see the first 20 chapters you were to learn to surrender, saturate, bless his name, trust in Him, praise during offence, heart to heart, renewed, strengthen, forgive, and so on to learn that you have to put aside your emotions. You were built to build the kingdom of God.

God is made up of many facets. He is a friend, provider, healer, comforter, a way maker. He will be what you need Him to be in your good and bad times. You can never just describe God as only having one attribute when he is comprised of so many wonderful attributes. It takes many ingredients to make a cake. Without flour you will not have a cake. Without Jesus' sacrificing for us on the cross we would not be able to claim his blood and have eternal life. It's all about Him!

Jesus came so that we could have life more abundantly. To have anything in life more abundantly, it has to be about Jesus. You can't have true happiness, peace, nor pleasure for a lifetime without Him. You can't lean on yourself or your family. It has to be all about Him. Oh, He wants you to have the best and to walk in abundance, but you have to give Him all of the glory. Your life does not belong to you, it belongs to Him.

When Jesus died for you, the exchange was made. His life for your life! Job *36:11 If they obey and serve him, they shall spend their days in prosperity and their years in pleasure.* Serve God in everything you do! That means when you go to the job that you may hate, serve God not man. Remember your attitude in everything that you do, you are heavily judged by the world and if you conform to the world's way of speaking, and acting, then the world will not come to Jesus by watching you.

God is looking at your behavior. You are the light in the earth, you are the ONLY representation that God has to show the world his goodness in the earth. *Matthew 5:16 Let your light so shine before men, that they may see your good works, and glorify your Father which is in heaven.* Your praise equips you with the strength and agility to allow God to shine through you each and every day.

Every morning is dedicated to God regardless of what you are going through emotionally, physically, or mentally. We all have tribulation, trials, and troubles that may hinder our praise, BUT remember to whom you belong and to whom you represent. Let people see the strength of God dwelling in your life. It's all about Him.

Your objective in this life is to live your best life with Christ. You have dual membership once you gave your life to Jesus. Your words are bound in heaven and in earth. God honors what you say in the earthly realm. That is why it is always important to watch what you say. Matthew *18:18 Verily I say unto you, Whatsoever ye shall bind on earth shall be bound in heaven: and whatsoever ye shall loose on earth shall be loosed in heaven.*

When you speak the angels go to work on behalf of the words that you have spoken. Your voice is important and holds valuable weight in the earth and in heaven. If God created the earth with just his words, and He has given you authority in the earth, speak life!

Don't miss this important opportunity to change and create an environment that represents the most high. God wants you to understand who you are and how important you are to Him. He wants you to live a beautiful life that includes Him in every area of your life. You have to acknowledge who He is and have faith in Him.

Being a Christian is more than just going to church, singing in a choir, ushering, and doing works. Your quality of life is important. Jesus bared everything at the cross so that you could live freely. There is a misconception that serving God is not pleasurable.

Jesus took all our iniquities at the cross, why not enjoy your life. Travel, go to the movies, purchase a beautiful home, live healthy and happy, but live the life that God has ordained you to have. Walk with a smile and allow the joy of the Lord to shine through you. Tell God every morning that you love Him. He is the reason you are able to be anything that you desire. It's all about Him.

Notes:_____

_____

_____

_____

_____

_____

_____

_____

_____

_____

_____

_____

_____

_____

_____

_____

_____

_____

_____

_____

_____

_____

_____

_____

_____

_____

Made in the USA
Middletown, DE
05 July 2015